PROUST'S WAY

Marcel Proust

PROUST'S WAY

by

FRANÇOIS MAURIAC

of The French Academy

Translated from the original French
"Du Côté de Chez Proust"

by

ELSIE PELL

PHILOSOPHICAL LIBRARY

NEW YORK

ISBN 978-0-8065-2967-7

Printed in the United States of America

TABLE OF CONTENTS

MY MEETING WITH
MARCEL PROUST

I saw Barrès for the last time at Marcel Proust's funeral. He was standing in front of the Church of Saint-Pierre de Chaillot, with his bowler on his head and his umbrella hanging from his arm. He was astonished at the clamor of fame all about the deceased whom he had known quite well and rather liked, I believe, without suspecting his greatness.

"Well, what's it all about! . . . he was our young man . . ." he kept repeating to me, meaning by that that he had always located Marcel Proust on the other side of the chancel with the worshipers and disciples, he the most intelligent and discerning of all, to be sure, and the one who knew how to burn the most flattering incense under the nose of every master; but that he would some day be able to bestride the Lord's Table and take his place along-side of him, that was something neither Barrès nor any other pontiff of his genera-tion would ever have foreseen.

"Ah! Proust, pleasant companion, what a strange phenomenon you were! as for me, what an off-hand way I had of judging you!" Barrès confessed to Jacques Rivière (letter of December 2, 1922 published in *Hommage à Marcel Proust*).

Proust concealed his own genius in the smoke of the incense-burner he was swing-ing under the noses of the men of letters and the ladies in whose homes he dined. Thanks to that cloud, he constructed his work for many years, borrowing anecdotes and secrets from the people whom he covered with flowers, growing fat on every destiny he crossed; and suddenly the cloud dispersed and "their young man," eternally young, towered above the dis-comforted old masters.

Some of them took it very badly (not

Barrès, to be sure, over whom a new work could not cast a shadow), but Bourget, who pretended to laugh at the maniac ("Crazy," he used to say to me, "to dissect flies' legs") was too discerning not to per- ceive that *Remembrance of Things Past* cast over his own novels a fearful shadow. That world of *Lies* (*Mensonges*), *A Wo- man's Heart* (*Un Coeur de Femme*), and *The Blue Duchess* (*La Duchesse bleue*) that Bourget had observed through his monocle, Proust, after having absorbed it, called forth from his depths, all mingled with his own life. What a drama was that sudden occupation of the literary heaven by the Proustian constellation! To be de- moted on the very threshold of his tomb with one foot already in the grave, was, perhaps what Bourget vaguely resented; but that is certainly what the Count Robert de Montesquiou felt desperately (as appears clearly in the last pages of his *Mémoires*). The latter lived long enough to discover that he would pass down to

3

posterity only in as far as it had pleased the little Proust to make use of him. What! That snob, mongrel, who drank the noble count in with his eyes and covered him with flattery, was concealing then an incorruptible witness, one of those geniuses who not only note the appearance, the gesture, the voice, but the hidden intention, and immobilize it in an eternal creation? Who would not have been deceived by it? Marcel Proust had nothing of the professional observer. He lived your life, admired you, liked you, took part in your follies and vices; he was a virtuoso in quarrelling and making up. But all the time that he lost with you was swallowed up in him, and he was to rediscover it later thanks to a "good use of illnesses" that Pascal had not foreseen.

There was one writer able to estimate the importance of Marcel Proust and to be overwhelmed by it, but without meanness or envy: it was the charming René Boylesve. He admitted without artifice that

Proust had accomplished what he himself had dreamed. He was not jealous of it, but confessed his sadness to us in the pretty little house on the rue des Vignes where I see again his handsome olive face, bearded and wasted away, one of those that give testimony equally to the excesses of penitence or the fires of human passions.

I saw Marcel Proust at the end of the war for the first time, at Madame Alphonse Daudet's, on the third of February 1918, during a reception given in honor of Francis Jammes. But I could have met him many years sooner since I was acquainted with Alphonse Daudet's youngest son, Lucien, who was not only one of Marcel Proust's best friends but had the merit to admire Marcel's genius at a time when nobody would have found himself in agreement with him. *Swann's Way* had hardly appeared in the bookstore windows when Lucien Daudet, in the *Figaro,* was already putting this unknown man and his work into their rightful place, at the top.

"That little Proust!" people kept saying, "do you really think that fellow exists?" Lucien Daudet never doubted that
the little Proust was very great; he never
put him down as commonplace. He resisted
that blindness of friendship that hides from
us the greatness of those we love, and he
belied *Swann's* author when the latter
assures us that we do not believe in the
genius of a person "with whom we went to
the opera last night." But why didn't he
ever speak to me about him? I keenly
sensed a presence, an influence, around
Lucien Daudet, a sort of shadow a bit
stifling that perhaps did harm to his own
expansion. As he often amused himself by
imitating the gestures and strutting of
Count Robert de Montesquiou, I thought
that it was by that person he was im-
pressed, and I blushed a little for him. But
Lucien Daudet, instead of confiding to me
that he had a brilliant friend to whom he
was going to introduce me, would an-
nounce to me for instance: "I am going to

do something very important for you; I am going to introduce you to the Marquise d'Ayragues."

* * * *

Under the influence of Balzac, I believed naively in the "Salons" as only a provincial can believe in them. I remember a dinner at the Duchess de Rohan's in 1910, in honor of Count Czernin, the Austrian ambassador. I do not know what had earned me that rapid promotion from the "poetic teas" of the good duchess where the strangest fauna of the Paris of that day assembled, to the great diplomatic dinner where, for the first time, I gazed in wonder at the parade of abundant and magnificent livery.

Perhaps it was that evening that I had the surprise of seeing Barrès in frock-coat wandering under the duchess' chandeliers. "I only came to meet that charming little Princess Bibesco," he said to me' "Have you read the *Huit Paradis?*"

The silhouette cut in the facet of his

eyeball, as Proust would have said, was always Astiné Aravian, a peri. This son of bleak Lorraine was forever searching in women for those angels of Asiatic nights that, in Paris, are disguised as princesses from the Balkans.

But it is of Proust that we must now speak. Although our mutual friends would never have thought of bringing us together, his existence and genius were revealed to me through the translation of *Sesame and Lilies* by Ruskin, for which Marcel Proust had written the preface. From the first lines of that preface, I felt myself on the frontier of an unknown country. How Gide could have had the manuscript of *Swann's Way* between his hands and not immediately been dazzled by it, is something I have never been able to understand, I whom that simple preface (it has been reprinted in *Pastiches et Mélanges* under the title *Une Journée de Lecture*) threw into a sort of stupor. From that moment I never stopped asking people about Proust and I was told about his strange secluded life into which I did not expect ever to penetrate. If I own a copy of the first printing of *Swann's Way,* it is because I had scarcely deciphered the name of Proust in the bookstore windows when I hastened to obtain the book.

But I had to wait until February 3, 1918 to meet the one living author whom I wished most to know. He seemed rather small to me, stoopshouldered in his tightfitting jacket, his thick black hair shadowing his pupils, dilated, it appears, by drugs. Stuffed into a very high collar, his starched shirtfront bulging like a breastbone, he cast on me a nocturnal eye whose intensity intimidated me. My confusion increased when, instead of the compliment I thought I saw forming on his lips, he let fly this epigram: "Francis Jammes dedicated a very pretty novelette to you. . . ." That was to make me understand that I had no other claim to his attention than that dedication. And yet I felt myself the object of an ex-

9

amination insistent though concealed.

Aside from that first interview, I had only a single occasion to speak at length with him, a few months before his death, one evening or rather one night when he invited me to dine at his bedside. And yet what ground had been covered between the first dedication: "To M. François Mauriac, in affectionate admiration . . ." and the last, on the flyleaf of *Sodom and Gomorrha*: "Dear François, how much admiration and also gratitude (especially admiration) I feel in writing you. But I have been *dead*. And I come up *de profundis* all bound up like Lazarus. I hope to see you soon. I could not reply to any of Jammes' books and yet you know how much he means to me. I am going to try to send this book to him. But life returns to me only drop by drop. Your friend Marcel Proust."

The same rapid evolution toward friendship is betrayed in the few letters that he addressed to me, either to thank me for an allusion made to his books in an article, or to speak to me of *La Chair et le Sang* and *Préseances,* the only novels of mine that he knew (unless the dedication quoted above refers to *The Kiss to the Leper*). Here they are in the order in which I think I received them, since they are not dated; according to the stamp on the envelope the first should be of September 24, 1919:

Dear Sir,

I can not tell you how touched I was by the two clippings I received. It is true that I do not answer articles, and this time there were only two adjectives. But they came from you.

Your friend, the master whom I admire above all, M. Francis Jammes, amidst end-less undeserved praises, had asked me to eliminate from the first volume of the work whose title I am so happy that you like, an episode that he considered shocking. I should have liked to be able to satisfy him. But I constructed that work so carefully that that episode in the first volume is the

11

explanation of the jealousy of my young hero in the fourth and fifth volumes, so that in tearing the column from the obscene capital I should later have caused the roof to cave in. That is what critics call works without composition and writings at the mercy of memories. Pardon me for speaking of myself in this way, but I thought confiding a method of work was a form of gratitude and an expression of sympathy.

Marcel Proust.

Dear friend,

You are so nice to me that I do not know how to thank you. I shall try to find a way. At the moment, I have bronchitis which keeps me in bed and prevents me even from writing letters. But however difficult it is for me to hold a pen because of the discomfort and fever, I was anxious to tell you that it is a joy for me to see your kind understanding grasp the slightest occasion this way. A clipping from the Figaro brings

12

me my gift and, thanks to the quotation you make "That there is no New Year's Day", forces me to note that, thanks to you, there is one just the same.

Marcel Proust.

Dear friend,

You're a monster (a nice one). I was going to write you because yesterday by accident someone showed me a review in which you delight me by comparing me to Carpentier, and honor me by comparing me to Claudel. And just at that moment a letter arrived in the mail signed Maurras. As he writes as illegibly as Léon Daudet (and that is really something), I thought he had not written himself (which astonished me) for the letter seemed fairly easy to decipher. Just the same, my unhappy eyes could not reach the end, but what I understood sufficed to make me think that it was not from Maurras. Then I took different glasses, then a magnifying-glass, and I read that Maurras was Mauriac. Your

13

letter would require such a long answer
that I am in no condition to undertake it.
What perversity, when I write you at a
moment when I would be unable to write
anyone how much I liked your book, to
say to me: "I feel that you did not like my
book because of its dramatic element."
What will you say when you read the last
volumes of mine, or at least those after the
novel about Albertine which I consider
dramatic? But since I am writing you to tell
you that I like your book, a black fuse that
destroys everything about it, why throw
my praises into confusion and destroy
them by criticism? Dear friend, I would
have a thousand amusing things to say to
you. But only one is important to me (not
amusing). You say to me: "Not an article
on my book." Do you want me to see to it
that they put one in the N. R. F. as soon
as your adversary Jacques Rivière comes
back from vacation? For some time past I
have had so little success that I scarcely
dare to propose that to you. You see, as

the latest blunder I made, I impulsively asked for an article on Jacques Boulenger's book. They promised me it would be charming, and it was so insulting that Jacques Boulenger sent a letter of correction in strong and unequivocal terms to the N. R. F. I sent a poem of Porel's also recommended by Fargue which was instantly refused, etc. Nevertheless, if you wish, I shall speak of it to Rivière as soon as he returns. Do you want me to ask l'Action Française which does not speak of me any more but will perhaps speak of you, passionate Spanish monk? Well, tell me what you want. (I can write to Chaumeix.)

What a nerve when I was dying, alas! not to live again, to write me: "Why do you want to see me once I have left for the country? How can I guess you have left for the country? I think you did not know my state of health. It seems to me I told you that I did not have the strength to correct my last book which was sent to the printer in the rough draft and was reread by

15

Gallimard, Rivière and Paulhan who were so kind in that matter. But it is all the same to you if one is dying. You are like the Belles-Lettres that reproach me for having scorned to send them my opinion of M. de Goncourt. And doubtless the Renaissance and other research reviews think that it is scorn, too. It is on account of that fatigue (after this letter I shall be two weeks without opening my eyes perhaps) that I do not propose to write an article for you myself (which, moreover, would offend so many masters and friends, whom I have had to refuse, as odd as it may seem for people to ask me for articles). I know you are very fond of Elie de Gaigneron (I, too. And if I have not seen him, it is because I have really been too ill) but do you like him to the degree that nothing can be said about him that you would not repeat to him? If not, I shall recount a rather amusing conversation that I had some time ago with him. (Conversation which does not concern you in any way and, moreover, is

in no way injurious to him.) *Do not think
any longer that if I do not like your books
I will wear myself out* (*in a state where
the words "wear out" no longer make any
sense*) *writing you that I like them. And
believe that I like you too. Your friend,*
                              Marcel Proust.

Here I shall spare the reader a letter in
which Marcel Proust comments at length
on *Le Livre de Saint Joseph* of his dear
Francis Jammes — a tiresome analysis
which ends on this note of meaningful am-
biguity: "I had many other subjects to
speak to you about, urgent and even out-
dated already, but serious because they
will, perhaps, cause two of your friends to
ask you to choose between them and me.
In which case I advise you warmly to
choose those who are your true and tried
friends, and whom you must not give up.
Besides, it is possible that they will not
give you this choice, and as you are very
certain that I shall not impose it, in that

case everything will be easy, at least in all that concerns us two."

A little later, Marcel Proust acknowl-edged the reception of my novel *Prése-ances*.

My dear, splendid friend, I wish my health permitted me to speak to you about that astonishing Préseances which is the most original, the most remarkable, the most unique book that I have read in a long time. If I am easily susceptible to the spirit of subtlety which differentiates a John Martineau from a Freddie Durand, to the painter's talent (sometimes a little exaggerated) that makes Hourtinat detest-able, even to the resources of the dramatic novelist which bring about the return of Augustin, with all that is mingled, or rather as a substructure to all that, there is an inner life that I am not very sure of understanding, and yet I want more than anything to love it.

Dear friend, and this has no close con-nection with what I just said to you, as a

18

rule I prize very little the conversational parts of books and see in them a lack of transposition. But when I hear your very pronunciation, when you are astounded or indignant, I bless you for bringing to life again the outlines of that evening when I had the pleasure of meeting you. (I mean the evening when you were kind enough to come to my little bedroom with my dear H., to-day departed for a distant land. . . .) Most certainly I have never stopped think-ing of your look, your voice, the things that you said, your letter the following day. But you gave to all that more precision and life when, in the form of printed words, I recognized that individually energetic and charming manner you have of saying the words. Your quotation from Chateau-briand, in its sublimity, brought me to the point of understanding why I was so at-tracted by certain consonants on certain pages. "To break with reality is nothing. But with memories. . . ."

Dear friend, I have not broken with the

memory of you and perhaps I shall even be permitted to see you otherwise than in the spirit and truth. I have been so deathly sick (I think I wrote you that I could not even correct my proofs and that the N. R. F. was nice enough to have my last volume published from the rough draft itself so that there were fewer mistakes in that book than in the others, for, as you say so very well, I do not know how to correct proofs) that I can not answer anyone or tire myself too much by asking you the meaning of certain pages of your book. Nothing that I like more and where I am reflected less; we must be very different from each other. To-day when everything is alike how unique your book is! I do not know how to correct proofs and still you should have sent me yours. I should have proposed the elimination of certain slight flaws.

If you see Francis Jammes tell him it is more than illness that keeps me from thanking him for Saint Joseph. I have just

20

remembered that when I did my military service at seventeen years of age (a unique case, I believe) in Orléans, there was a lieutenant in the regiment, so nice, of such inordinate courtesy, small, thin, dark, with a very pretty face, that he went about in the streets of Orléans wih a huge prayer-book under his arm. At the time it was very courageous. I am told that he died that same year. People wept when they spoke of him. I wonder if he was a relative of Francis Jammes. May that great poet, through your intercession, recommend me to his favorite saint, so that he may bestow an easy death on me although I feel that I have ample courage to face a very cruel one. Faithfully yours,

Marcel Proust.

P.S.—I am going to start to get up again occasionally and go out a bit these days, in spite of the unfortunate results of my recent experience. Perhaps we could take advantage of this so as to see each other. The trouble is that I know so late when I can get up that by that time I shall not know where to get you. I saw that Francis Jammes was presenting himself to the Academy. In regard to this matter, some-one related to me a conversation of your friend M. Arthur Meyer, a conversation that alarmed me by the heedless idiocy of many society people. I thought I saw the director of the Gaulois with his rosy sugar-loaf pate of the great pontiff of the Belle Hélène, and on his neck, as the Goncourts would have said, the frizzly curls of a lap-dog, proclaiming his prophecies in a nasal voice. Besides, I don't know why I make fun of him; I "guermantised"* the other evening, and my pleasantest hosts ap-peared to me just as stupid. Dear friend, I can not make up my mind to leave you.

Here is the last letter I received from Marcel Proust.

---

* To act like Guermantes. Verb formed from the name of one of Proust's most important characters, the Duke of Guermantes, an affected, aristocratic member of the old regime. Translator's note.

Dear friend, you guessed, did you not, that since your visit I have been seriously ill. Had it not been for that, would I have been able to refrain from writing you, in spite of your request and even without waiting for your letter? I am sending you this word at a time when I am still suffering. But I do not want my continued silence to make you think I have dreamed of forgetting you. When we see each other again, if we do see each other, I beg you, be just as you tell me you generally are. I can not understand that the admiration you tell me you have for me can change anything, since you know that there is, on my side, an equal and reciprocal admiration. So they neutralize one another, and we should see each other as two gay men who love life (even the one who is half dead) and who, when they are alone and separate think deeply, but together engage in all the kinds of amusement of good folk who are not artists and who do not admire each other, amusements from which liter-

ary conversations are, of course, not neces-
sarily excluded.

I am so tired I tell you all that very badly
with a pedantic air that fills me with hor-
ror, and as if you did not know as well and
better than I what constitutes the charm
of frank and simple friendships.

Cordially yours,

Marcel Proust.

Here I should recount an incident which
preceded that nocturnal repast at Marcel
Proust's bedside and to which there is ref-
erence in a letter. The night before, I received this message by telephone: "Marcel
Proust would like to know whether M.
François Mauriac would care to hear the
Capet String Quartet during the meal or
whether he prefers to dine with the Count
and Countess of X. . . ."

To-day I would not have hesitated to
catch the dear mystifier in his net, and I
would have demanded the Capet Quartet,
but in my persistent innocence, I was pro-

24

fuse in my gratitude and answered that I wished nothing and nobody except the presence of Marcel Proust himself. This little fact ends by throwing light on certain aspects of that strange man, the same that the letters which he addresses to me betray. Even if we knew nothing of Marcel Proust, those letters would suffice to recreate a character like the greater part of those that populate his novel. For instance, under that flood of civilities, that interpretation of my wail: "Not an article on my book . . ." which he translates immediately as a disguised request, that deluge of words to refuse me what I am not asking for, the bait of tittle-tattle in regard to G. he throws to me, or again that allusion to friends who would force me to choose be- tween them and him, all that in spite of a sincere sympathy and a touching sweet- ness, exhales a rather offensive odor, that of the society whose hell he describes to us. In the depths of that sick man, attacked at the meeting-place of flesh and spirit, the

outside world against which he was defenseless, which was swallowed up in him
and which his memory brought up again,
bathed for years. All those characters
were immersed in it, as it were, and under-
went alterations due to that physiological
bath.

My admiration for Marcel Proust
twenty years after his death remains just
as lively but is, nevertheless, slightly al-
tered. I am not as certain that the work,
in its entirety, marks the triumph of a
method. This strikes me: the heights of
that great work emerge from the most distant past of the author. Only the child in
Swann's Way and the grown-up people
that the child observed with an unspoiled
gaze (I am thinking in particular of the
famous episode: One of Swann's loves)
have resisted corruption.

But as the time recaptured by Proust
moves away from his early years and
brings to the surface a determined sexual

life and the beings it drags along behind it, the metal of the work, up to then intact, is corroded little by little. It resists in certain places as though preserved by the sacred memory of the mother and grandmother of the hero. Everywhere else, the corruption of a life, stagnant though remarkably attentive, defenseless against the outer world, given over entirely to swarming sensations, besieges, penetrates, gnaws and destroys the human beings to whom the novelist had given existence. In the last volumes, even the face of Françoise, the immortal servant, fades out. The phantom of Albertine floats like ectoplasm in the suffocating darkness of a room. With the living gone, nothing remains except the incomparable clinical study of jealousy in an accursed creature to whom the love that God has showered upon human couples is forbidden. Everything that was flesh in the novel gives way little by little to corruption and returns to dust, but the framework remains: those views, those generali-

27

zations of the most *profound* moralist who has ever existed in any literature.

That is to say that Proust's work appears to me just as dominating as twenty years ago. I stand amazed at discovering that its importance still escapes certain critics. Proust's place in the ranks of the great European novelists will never be taken away from him. It remains for us to find ourselves to-day more sensitive than we were in the dazzlement of first reading, to that contamination of a whole romantic world by that morbid creator who bore it too long mingled with his own life, mixed with his deep murkiness, and who communicated to it the germs with which he found himself infected.

In the course of the night that Marcel Proust reminds me in a letter, when the Capet Quartet did not play, I recall that gloomy room on the rue Hamlin, that black den, that bed where an overcoat served as a blanket, that waxy mask through which it could have been said our

28

host watched us eat, and whose hair alone seemed living. As for him, he no longer partook of the nourishment of this world. The hidden enemy of which Baudelaire speaks, that time "which consumes life" and which "grows and strengthens itself on the blood we lose" was condensing, materializing at the bedside of Proust, already more than halfway to non-existence, and was becoming that enormous, proliferous mushroom, nourished on his own substance, his work: *Le Temps retrouvé*.

He still made use of the language of friendship in which he had not believed for a long time. Woe to the man who can not distinguish between tenderness and desire! Woe to the heart incapable of cherishing another heart, without the flesh being attacked and wounded! The words he still used no longer corresponded to that inner havoc, that destruction. The formulas of tenderness survived only on lips all dried up by a frightful thirst which would never be quenched.

29

Yet in his evocation of that nocturnal repast, he names: "My incomparable H." But the boy was to leave a short time afterwards for America where Proust had found him a situation. And so he cut the last moorings; and he remained alone in that furnished room, worrying about the proofs of his book, the paste-ons that he added in the margins, between two choking fits, having no other connection with his friends than the one which binds him to them now that he is no longer there. His relationships with us were a forerunner of those that death establishes between a writer and his admirers who can reach him no longer except through his books.

And certainly Proust is as living in my eyes as many of those who have survived him — as living as Jean Cocteau whose route crosses mine at long intervals, and whom I recognize by his voice, by that very slight squint, by that skinny hand, by that delicate lizard's foot that in 1910 he held up with the same gesture in the dark entrance of his house on rue d'Anjou, before the eyes of an astonished valet de chambre, as when, in the salon of Madam Alphonse Daudet, he recited in an affected and charming tone:

> *My brothers of Paris, our divine realm*
> *Spreads out in all directions from*
> *the Place Vendome*

A Cocteau before Diaghilew, before the discovery of *Paludes* at Offranville at Jacques-Emile Blanche's home, before Apollinaire, Max Jacob and Picasso, before the illumination that determined his fame.

At this crossroads where I have arrived, I hesitate between a thousand trails. It is not a life that I am recounting. The most uniform existence, the least filled with events, the most sedentary, is a cloth so closely woven with circumstances and passions, so many other destinies cross it, it is a skein so tangled that even if we were deprived of all shame, that would be of no

31

use to us except to resolve us to say everything.

The youth of a man appears short on
the plane of eternity, but under the micro-
scope that drop of water discloses a swarming comparable to that of the infinite
spaces. The integral history of a young
life, of its loves, its friendships, its weak-
nesses, its intellectual or religious crises,
offers the vast proportions of the history of
the ideas and customs at a certain epoch
as they are reflected in a single spirit. And
a long old age would not be enough to
complete the account or to exhaust its
drama.

ONE OF PROUST'S CHARACTERS

The *Mémoires* of the Count de Montes-quiou will not do honor to his memory. What a lesson to see a gentleman whose knowledge of the world was, so to speak, his specialty, fall so naively into the trap of the other world! Nothing more likely to do us a disservice than those carefully drawn-up effusions of our posthumous writings, those little belated revenges, that tremen-dous admiration we measure out shame-lessly for our character and works. It would lead one to believe that the thought of death kills the fear of ridicule in us. Should the Count de Montesquiou be judged by his *Mémoires?* Was he merely the major-domo of trivial pleasures, that ancestral tapestry weaver of all the faddists who to-day profess "to arrange interiors," that esthete of undeniably bad taste, that old

33

gentleman who did not spare the old ladies, that embittered poet, famished for incense, who brings to us almost nothing of all his famous friends except flattering and, more-over, purely conventional letters that he received from them?

If that had been all he was, we would have great difficulty in understanding why various distinguished young men of the generation that followed him admired him so much, admired him to such a degree that, never having had the honor of meet-ing the Count de Montesquiou, I am per-suaded that I knew him, I have seen his disciples copy his bearing and his swagger-ing so slavishly. For the count made a liar of La Bruyère who thought that "scorn and swaggering in society bring exactly the contrary results from what one is looking for, if that is to make oneself respected." M. de Montesquiou charmed by that very haughtiness; he offered a timely interest, and if he did not imitate the ways of Lau-zun, at least he possessed his manners. The mingling of American and Jewish blood renders almost obsolete in the world of to-day this combination of elegance, wit, conceit, insolence and fashion whose secret the Count de Montesquiou had inherited, but which the knowledge that he had of history permitted him to bring to such a high degree of perfection. No one knew better than he how to brush up his character and retouch it after such and such a model studied in the *Mémoires*. An esthete on the scent of all the horrors that "modern style" invented, his natural taste ran to pink palaces and Trianons for which he was evidently made. We easily imagine him in the queen's coterie, among the Polignacs, the Adhémars, the Besenvals, the Vaudreuils, capable of lampooning his sovereign scurvily, but perhaps also of dying for her. And finally, he was one of the last French gentlemen who deserved the epithet of ostentatious, one of the last who knew how to give banquets. ("Do you count on giving banquets?" I was asked haughtily by

one of the Count de Montesquiou's admirers whom I was telling I had rented three
tiny rooms on the fourth floor without ele-
vator.) The account of those solemnities
occupies so much space in the *Mémoires*
that it seems likely the noble count perhaps
saw in them the least perishable part of his
work. In respect to them, he divided humanity into two camps, the elect and the
excluded, two terms of which you must
think at once when you are trying to de-
fine snobism. Never say: "I am not a snob."
You will be very close to becoming one the
day you are one of the blessed "elect" as
the Count de Montesquiou calls his guests.
If, indeed, on some other occasion you are
among the "excluded," you risk, if not suffering, at least bad-humor. Snobism begins
with this inclination toward bad-humor.
To elect, to exclude, that is the double
movement of aspiration and expiration by
which the worlds subsist, as do the acad-
emies and clubs. So the wise man will es-
tablish himself as far as possible from the

zone where he risks being drawn in, then rejected, for there is nothing more shame-ful than to suffer for base causes.

Yet, just as Pliny the Elder perished for having wished to observe the eruption of Vesuvius at close range, so it is admirable that our Proust threw himself into the jaws of the monster to give us an accurate pic-ture, and that he, in a certain degree, in-noculated himself with snobism to know it better. Behold! Proust's name, which I hesitate to write here, is escaping me. The Count de Montesquiou would doubt-less have made a great outcry if they had predicted to him at that time that he would exist for us only as an adjunct of Proust. He died late enough to feel some fear, as is proven by a long, bitter and even venom-ous note added to his *Mémoires in extremis* (March 1920). What does Proust owe to his friend? A witness who knew both of them well, Jacques-Emile Blanche, assures me that neither Proust, the man, nor his work would have been what they were without Montesquiou. But is it right to speak of influence? Several of Proust's friends have helped us to understand his half-unconscious way of absorbing what each person was capable of furnishing him. He never let anyone go away without having extracted from him everything that could nourish his work, and it is certain that the Count de Montesquiou must have been wonderfully profitable to him. He was doubtless the great collector who made millions of traits, pieces of gossip and ana, by which his knowledge of the world was enriched, trickle down to the novelist. And it is even possible that Proust especially owes it to his noble friend that he took the world seriously, believed in its reality, gave it, if we may say so, a certificate of existence. For to-day, if all that has been unduly ennobled and all of the American and Jewish that is mixed in should be skimmed off, would enough of that high aristocratic French society of the Guermantes remain to write another work called *Remembrance of Lost Aristocracy?*

And lastly, the Count de Montesquiou furnished Proust with certain traits—certain ones only—for the character of a great lord lost among us. Let us take care in this not to confuse with that rather soiled creature, just as one did not confuse him formerly with des Esseintes, a noble poet, often inspired, who never sacrificed real and personal grandeur to what Madame de Lambert called "the grandeur of institutions,"—who rendered the last agony of Verlaine more bearable, and also that of one of Stéphane Mallarmé's children, who served the memory of Marceline Desbordes-Valmore,—and who had a very high opinion of friendship, although at the same time he seems to have had a prodigious virtuosity for getting mixed up in quarrels.

AT THE TOMB
OF MARCEL PROUST

In that furnished room, before the admirable sleeping face of Marcel Proust, we
were meditating on the extraordinary destiny of a creator whom his creation devoured.

Marcel Proust gave his life that his work
might live, and that is without precedent;
for Balzac's creditors chained him to his
table with financial worries. Proust separated himself from the world only to construct a world. Illness doubtless aided that
renunciation, but it could just as well have
inclined him toward the pursuit of luxury,
easy companionships and a soft life that
would have distracted him from his illness.

Between the bare walls where he reposes, we understand at last that strange
asceticism, that total stripping off of everything that was not his work and which

went so far as the refusal of all nourishment, when he was persuaded that fasting
would aid in his recovery, would leave him
respite to achieve at length that heroic and
mad pursuit of "things past."

During the last night, he was still dictating reflections on death, saying: "That
will serve for Bergotte's death." And on
the envelope stained with infusion, we saw
the last illegible words that he traced,
where the only decipherable thing was the
name of Forcheville; and so, up to the end,
his creatures will have been nourished on
his substance, will have exhausted what-
ever life he had left in him.

In that cell of a terribly commonplace
"furnished-room" face to face with the
body of a man of letters who loved letters
enough to die for them, we recalled Pascal's
prayer asking God for a good use of illnesses. How should an infirmity of the
body be used? Marcel Proust, as weak and
suffering as Pascal, having asked himself
the question just as he did, answered as he

41

did by the complete gift. To be sure, he made wonderful use of illness; but instead of using it as did Pascal, to seize that which endures, he used it to seize that which passes. Only in the midst of his suffering, he drew from himself in some way, during his life of retirement, that universe that he had absorbed during his public life. He not only peopled it with numerous beings at all stages of their existence, social, sentimental, sexual; but he also captured days, moments, a turn in the road at a certain hour of a certain year, and in that almost sordid room, he suddenly rediscovered and made fast, like a living butterfly, the perfume of a hedge of hawthorn.

In this way sprang up, by dint of suffering, the immense forest of his work where a single name: Swann, Combray, Guermantes swelled out like a clearing from which branched off roads that numerous by-paths joined together. Proust, with sublime patience, tried in this superhuman task, between beings and landscapes, between their names and the forms, sounds, colors, perfumes, to exhaust the correspon' dency, suppress the intervals, and finally to construct a living symphony. Bergson wrote that the entire past follows us at every instant: "What we have felt, thought, wished since our early childhood is there, hovering over the present which is going to join it, pressing against the door of consciousness that would like to leave it outside. . . ." Marcel Proust's endeavor went in exactly the opposite direction of the cerebral mechanism of other men who have the tendency to push every useless memory aside into the unconscious. His consciousness was, on the contrary, trained by him not to mistrust memories, to snatch up every reminiscence in passing. Not that he let the flood of bygone days be dis' gorged without control; there is not a char' acteristic in *Remembrance of Things Past* that was not chosen from among a thou' sand; but Marcel Proust's choice deals with his whole past.

43

Do you see that man alone, struggling step by step until death against the mount-ing flood of memories, that weak Hercules who captures the flow of time, or wisely abandons himself to the ebb-tide? He died of that maddening work; he died perhaps without God whose love would have turned him from it, as it turned Pascal from all human goals. For us, his younger brothers who loved and admired him, that is a terrible lesson he leaves us: art is not a joke; it concerns life and it concerns much more. Marcel Proust, in spite of his Gon-court Prize, never had a career, and it was probably only during his last five years that he saw the sun of his fame rise and shine. But the greater part of his human life was passed between the cork-lined walls of an apartment on the Boulevard Haussmann, and no one at that time, ex-cept a few friends, foresaw what was being born there in travail, the most powerful romantic work of the era. Proust had the strength to see reputations made, quick

44

fame arise and still never to relinquish the treasure that he was amassing unknown to us. Yet we recall our admiration when, at the age of twenty, we read that preface he wrote for *Sesame and Lilies* by Ruskin. That single fragment permitted us to perceive the unknown deposits that a recluse had just discovered.

We have faith in the perennity of that work. Without doubt, it will always be a small number who will love to lose themselves in the enchanted forest, so mysterious and yet so wittingly drawn; an elite who will take pleasure in the detours, the entanglements, the dead-end roads, the ill-defined stopping places. But just as the whole world admires *Manon Lescault* which is only one seventh of the Memoirs of a man of quality, the general public has already known how to cut out fragments from Proust's work, such as *One of Swann's loves*, *A Death-Struggle* and *The Intermittence of the Heart*.

Shall we proceed to the end of the reflections which beset us face to face with that great man, we should say, that great sleeping young man? (For on his deathbed, you wouldn't have thought him fifty years old, but scarcely thirty, as if time had not dared to touch the one who had mastered and conquered it.) Will we dare to say everything? His hands were not joined, but his arms floated like those of the vanquished; the crucifix was not resting on the motionless breast. Does such a work, we were thinking, imply even the renunciation of God? God is terribly absent from Marcel Proust's work. We are not of those who reproach him for having penetrated into the flames, into the rubbish of Sodom and Gomorrha; but we deplore the fact that he ventured there without adamantine armor. From the literary point of view alone, it is the weakness of that work and its limitation; the human conscience is absent from it. Not one of the beings who people it is acquainted with moral anxiety, or scruple, or remorse, or desires perfection.

46

Scarcely a one who knows what purity means; or else the pure, like the mother or grandmother of the hero, are so without knowing it, as naturally and effortlessly as the other characters who sully themselves. It is not the Christian who judges here; the lack of moral perspective impoverishes the humanity created by Proust, narrows its universe. The great mistake of our friend appears to us less in the boldness, sometimes hideous, of a part of his work than in what we would call in a word, the absence of Grace. To those who follow him, for whom he has marked out a trail toward unknown lands and whom, with desperate audacity, he has caused to brush against continents submerged under dead seas, it remains to reintegrate Grace into this new world.

There then is the man of letters in his paroxysm, the one who made an idol of his work and whom the idol devoured. It was not for him a distraction from his pain, since he nourished it on that very pain,

47

since he enriched it with priceless medita-
tions on insomnia, fever, dreams, sleep, on
the approach of death and the last agony
(and there this descendant of Stendhal,
Flaubert and Balzac plunges his roots
down to Montaigne). And so this devour-
ing work probably turned him from the
Infinite Being alone. . . . But yet, do we
know that? It is not sufficient to say of
such a monument that it was a necessity;
we have the right to recognize there a particular will of God. And then, let us recall
what Marcel Proust suffered. As he suffered for years without dying, his friends
found it convenient and reassuring sometimes to smile at it. Proust's nocturnal life
seemed to them a peculiarity of the hypo-
chondriac and they would not see anything
but sallies in the allusions to his death, in
the moaning which crops up in all his letters: "I wanted to write you, but I have
been dead. And I come up *de profundis*
all bound like Lazarus."

In another, he calls himself "he who is

already dead," and in regard to Jammes: "May that great poet, through your inter- cession, recommend me to his favorite saint so that he will give me an easy death, al- though I feel that I have sufficient courage to face a very cruel one. . . ."

But it is precisely in that prayer for the good use of illnesses, of which we were speaking at the beginning, that Pascal sends up this cry: "O God, Who loves so dearly bodies that suffer! . . ." Therefore Marcel Proust was loved, and we believe that to- day he sees, smiling and alive at his ap- proach, the stone cortege he admired so much at the church-door of Balbec: "The apostles . . . on both sides of the Virgin be- fore the deep bay of the porch were await- ing me as though to do me honor. The kindly face, snub-nosed and gentle, the stooped shoulders, seemed to advance with an air of welcome chanting the *alleluia* of a beautiful day. . . ."

PROUST'S VIEW
OF LOVE

The two volumes of *La Prisonnière*
(*The Captive*) forces us to revise our opinion of Proust's work to a certain degree.
We thought that our friend, in making use,
moreover, of an entirely different method,
wished, like Balzac, to compete with the
registry office. And without a doubt he
found within himself enough living beings
to justify that pretension. But those beings
whom he had absorbed at the time of his
worldly life and then restored to the light
at the time of his sequestered life while he
was making use of his illness for patient research, were never entirely detached from
himself, the most diverse resembled each
other, because they resembled him. Between Swann's love for Odette, that of
Saint-Loup for Rachel, and Marcel's for

Gilberte and Albertine, there is no differ-
ence in nature; it is the same sort of love,
but one of whose ravages Proust makes
us aware in his first books as a novelist,
while in *La Prisonnière*, he studies them almost abstractly as a clinician. Those characters that used to divert him so much
seem to interest him less and less. Issuing
from him without the thread ever having
been broken, they reenter him and are lost
in his shadow. Hard pressed by illness,
choking with all that he still has to say to
us before going away, Marcel Proust feels
less complacency for his creatures and sees
only that they interpose themselves between him and us. Just as in the last year
of his life, he brushed aside his dearest
friends, so, perhaps, he bore up uneasily
this living world of his books.* For the first
time, in *La Prisonnière*, he gives the name
of Marcel to his hero, he resolutely occupies the center of the stage. The contours

---

*The two volumes of *Albertine disparue* (*The Sweet Cheat
Gone*) that we possess to-day weaken this judgment. From the
romantic point of view alone, they are admirable, perhaps because
they were not touched up during the author's last illness.

51

of his best drawn characters become less clearly defined. When Françoise says to him, "Right now, your snow-white pajamas, as you move your neck, make you look like a dove . . ." we do not recognize the familiar voice of Combray's old servant. And, without a doubt, we find here a Charlus more pronounced than in the preceding volumes, a frightful Charlus, too frightful! He is not a sick person; he is the sickness. We make the acquaintance of a cancer patient and we see nothing but the cancer. That secretive Charlus of the first books, whose disease was betrayed only by a look, a flower, or a too vivid handkerchief, here breaks out, bursts, runs like an abscess that would never stop emptying itself. To tell the truth, nothing in *La Prisonnière* is so important to Proust as revealing to us the result of his investigations concerning love. It is only in the study of feeling that he worries about being veracious and, to the necessities of that study, he subordinates his narration, twists events

52

without regard to verisimilitude. We accept the fact that a young society girl like
Albertine comes to live with a young man
alone; but the author should render cred-
ible to us such an extraordinary contin-
gency, show us the reasons and conse-
quences. He should . . . but let us hasten to
say that, entirely occupied with the terrible
discoveries in which Proust enlists us, we
let ourselves be overtaken by his indiffer-
ence for everything that is not that im-
placable research. And besides, so much
the worse, if the others exist less, since he
is there always, more living than he ever
was, motionless in his bed. But in spite of
the sealed windows all of life revolves
around that extended body. He approaches
it, tames it, captures the cries from the
street, the sun's darts, the trickling of the
rain. As he does with Albertine, he draws
the universe into his sick chamber and
holds it prisoner. Proust alone suffices for
this research where we travel in his train,
to that height in a pitiless light where,

overcome by dizziness, we hold fast to his cloak.

Under the name of love, Proust has always designated the suffering that the relationships, known or guessed, or supposed, or divined, of the beloved being with other beings causes him. His erotic activity leads him into maneuvres, investigations, an immense game of espionage that complicates still more the sickly state of the cloistered lover. The alcove stirs like the office of an examining magistrate. To put on the screws, the judge shuts up the accused Albertine in his office and holds her under his thumb; she leaves only under escort. Alas, the past would suffice to exercise the clairvoyance of the lover, for his terrible memory never forgives the perfidy of any contradiction in her remarks; but there are sorties that render suspect the complicity of Andrée, friend in every extremity, and that of the too complacent chauffeur. What could be called "the inquest on jealousy," although shown here in its paroxysm, retains a character of generality that assures Proust the first place among all the masters of jealousy. Let us open the book at random: "One arrives, in the form of suspicions, at absorbing daily, in enor-mous doses, that same idea that one is be-ing deceived, of which a very small quan-tity could be fatal, inoculated by the needle of a cutting word." "Two are not necessary, it is enough to be alone in your room thinking, for new betrayals of your mistress to occur, even if she were dead." What a collection of admirable maxims could one not extract from this book for the profit of busy people!

But in *La Prisonnière*, at the same time that the analysis goes further and deeper, it becomes restricted, limited, until it is no more than the study, though extraordi-narily suggestive, of one case, of an excep-tion. In proportion as the jealous lover, the jailor of the beloved, has less pretext for suffering, he no longer feels love; he does not love any more. It is necessary for Al-

55

bertine to torture or worry him. As soon
as he feels assured that she has not tried to
join a friend at the Trocadero or the Ver-
durins', Marcel himself has no longer any
other desire than to be alone. He is no
longer hungry for that flesh as soon as he
believes no one is stealing it from him
and that it is not escaping his desire.
Albertine takes a great deal of trouble to
hide her betrayals, and she does not understand that they are the only thing that hold
her lover and that, hardly has he been re-
assured, when there he is indifferent. The
one who has suffered so much because this
body belonged to others, now that all that
is released to him without sharing it, seems
to lose even the instinct of that possession,
even at the moment of pleasure itself. To
be sure he knows how to steal from that
sleeping body a clandestine partial pleasure, but the nightly caress is only the ap-
peasement of his suspicions; it takes its
stand between the sedative and the sopo-
rific. He does not seem to conceive of plea-

sure as an effort to lose ourselves in the
cherished object, to become one with it,
and finally to render vain its supreme and
involuntary treason of being another than
ourselves. Does he try to bring that soul
close to him? Fortuny's pearls and precious
materials are only rude means of making
the cage bearable for the poor bird. For
want of being able to possess Albertine in
her past and her future, in all the intervals
of space and time that she has occupied
and will occupy, for want of realizing an
impossible possession, this lover loses interest in the only possible possession,* and
sends up that admirable and forlorn cry:
"How does any one have the courage to
want to live, how can any one make a
movement to preserve himself from death
in a world where love is provoked only by
falsehood, and consists only of our need to
see our sufferings appeased by the being

---

*Impossible, for the beloved being is not one but multiple. How
possess what continues? One personality, in the beloved being, suc-
ceeds another indefinitely. You might as well want to immobilize a
river, stop its flow. In that lies the vanity of every conquest. It is
with his conception of human personality that a profound criticism
of Proust should deal.

who has made us suffer?" Proust ought to
have added, so that his entire conception
of love might be summed up in this sen-
tence: "A world where the beloved being
is no longer loved as soon as he no longer
makes us suffer." It would remain only to
admire and be silent, if Proust did not
claim for the love that he has just analyzed
a universal character. Proust does not seem
to doubt here that it is a question of not
only one kind of love, but of love. And it
is on this point, it seems to us, that there
would, perhaps, be objections to propose
to him. Perhaps . . . but this love in which
our executioner is the very one from whom
we await comfort is called unrequited
love; and if it is true that that is the most
common kind among poor humanity shall
we deny that Marcel Proust knew how, in
La Prisonnière, to rejoin the universal?

FROM MARCEL PROUST
TO JACQUES RIVIÈRE

Jacques Rivière was Marcel Proust's witness as he was Claudel's and Gide's. I take the word "witness" here in its absolute sense. He witnessed the action of each of those writers on a French youth who surrendered himself to them, and as he would have observed the advance of a poison in his own veins, he observed the changes brought about by each master in his conception of man and of life.

But what makes his meeting with Marcel Proust particularly interesting, is the time of his life when it took place; on his return from captivity which had been a time of abandonment to God, when he had no other occupation than to note His traces in his heart. Proust was, if not the agent of a conversion in reverse, at least from the time of Jacques' re-entrance into normal life, the most exalting example of a total submission to what is, to be sure, not against all religious law, but outside of and in ignorance of all metaphysics.

Jacques was the witness whom we influenced (even the beginner that I was as can be seen from the letters I am publishing) and who permitted himself to be "influenced" all the more because he recognized his power to defend himself and reject the work by which he had been penetrated and nourished for a time. He embraced an author so tightly, with a passion at once submissive and lucid, only because he never doubted that he would stifle him some day and throw him away like useless rubbish.

But all that will be developed later. What is important to notice is that the bringing together of Proust and Rivière in this little book is not artificial, in spite of what separates this sick man devoured by his past, this amazing leper, this heart full of precipices and abysses, from the Bordeaux youth with his clear childlike look who had understood everything before the others but took pleasure in nothing, and especi' ally women, until many years after the others were already satiated and disgusted.

ANIMA NATURALITER
CHRISTIANA

Of a modest nature and, in certain ways,
so secretive, Jacques Rivière had, nevertheless, drawn us all along into the quest
and discovery of his secret. Others might
have wished to know themselves with the
same passion; no one did it so openly as
Rivière; he was such a persevering, pene-
trating critic only because he needed his
masters and all his comrades, in order to go
down deeper into his heart; but he never
alienated anything from himself. His privi-
lege of seeing directly into the minds of
creatures, that admirable gift, deceived
some people. They thought that such
knowledge of others, such lucid adherence
to certain men, to certain works, must be
the sign of an utter abandonment. As a
matter of fact, his greatness—perhaps his

misfortune—was not to be able to be anyone's disciple; he never attained anything
—even the immutable—that he did not
resolve to surpass it. He submerged himself in a work, but like the diver who
swims directly toward what he is looking
for, then, with a single stroke, comes up
to the surface and tries to reach the bank,
he goes away without turning his head.
Thanks to the yeast of Claudel and Gide,
there fermented in him extreme and in-
compatible sentiments thenceforth sub-
missive to his control. Gide helped him
free himself from Claudel and Péguy;
Claudel and Péguy from Gide; Proust and
Freud pulled him away from the other
three, and already, I observed by certain
signs, he was beginning to drop Proust. He
no longer needed those masters whom he
never stopped loving and admiring; he had
gotten from them everything he could as-
similate. In the eternal effort to "create his
soul just as it is," he burned up everything
that was the object of his acquaintance

63

and pious love. Even in friendship, though
he never ceased to cherish his friends, he
departed when his integrity seemed to be
in danger: "What a difficult task it is to
fulfill oneself! How many bonds must be
snapped! How many contacts broken!
How alone is the man within whom stirs
the pitiful and imperious duty to create!"
"I am frightfully autonomous," he wrote
me one day. That is the truth; he never
submitted to any other law than his own,
but how strictly he imposed it on himself!
A hard law, which nothing could resemble
less than Gide's dizzy play between
Heaven and Hell. Rivière's entire effort,
during those last years, seemed to be opposed to his profound tendencies. That
Christian tried to become a Greek again
(in the Nietzschian sense); he had erected
his critical barriers, formerly thrown down
at the time of penitence, kneeling and tears.
He bent every effort to destroy that
higher nature toward which Christianity
obliges us to aspire; no longer holiness,

64

but simple wisdom and adaptation to life, no longer infinite aspiration, but content, ment within the limitations of the senses and the mind. He had conceived a horror for the drama, the kind that is superadded to inner conflicts to magnify them, to make something interesting out of them. He persuaded himself that what people call pleasure or happiness, if one could manage to attain it, is the most interesting thing that exists in the whole world. In this way Rivière took sides against his soul. It was in vain, he wrote to me, that he felt ashamed of all the time lost in believing happiness impossible; nothing could prevent him from belonging for all eternity to that race to whom what men call happiness is not happiness but "that thing which takes the place of happiness" as it is written in *Partage de Midi*. It is entirely a question of knowing whether a Christian heritage put into us that excessive exigency that Rivière tries to destroy, superadded it to our nature, whether Christian educa-

65

tion exasperates it, whether the church wisely encourages an appetite that she alone knows how to satisfy (and then Rivière would have been able to root out of himself, eliminate the poison), or whether, on the contrary, that exigency is consubstantial in us to such a point that the men of antiquity, before Christ came, felt the torment of that thirst that only He can assuage.

Is there an essential conformity between the Revelation and the nature of man? If that conformity exists, who better than our Rivière would have recognized it, he "whom no ruin could distract from his mania for attention and who threw him-self upon the worst misfortunes as upon an object of prey?" Indeed, he did recognize it, especially during the years of war and his captivity when so much misery gave him knowledge of the Cross. But let us re-call Pascal's cry: "How many natures in man's nature! How many vocations!" That is the trap in which Rivière seemed to be caught: that taste for tallying antagonistic vocations within him; the worst of it is that such a method forced him to lose on the two boards; for at the same time that he forbade himself to approach God, human happiness escaped his pursuit: that passion for love that such a mania for analysis does not destroy, doubtless, that it even excites, but above all paralyzes, that it defrauds of conquest and of satisfaction.

"To die," he moaned, "to yield to that monstrous combination of sentiments that occupies my heart, and that I shall never know how to unknot. . . ." If we knew a being perfectly, we should, without doubt, be warned when his death is approaching. I am thinking of all my friends whom that alone could cure: to pass on to life eternal. One day Jacques Rivière wrote me: "I feel myself too forsaken." He by Whom he thought himself forsaken was approaching his body and soul in a terrible way; unknown to him, He was preparing them. Among so many reasons that should have inspired joy and pride in him, our friend felt a strange detachment without sadness; he said repeatedly that only his wife and children held him here.

However detached he was, we know how much that break with the world cost him. Perhaps Jacques Rivière had to know such martyrdom to be able to send out that great cry of deliverance as the priest who had given him absolution was going away: "And now I know I am miraculously saved."

ON THE TRAIL
OF GOD

A writer who stiffened himself all his life
into one attitude, leaves behind him, after
his death, an official image which no one
would dream of retouching. But an author
whose concern was to be sincere toward
himself, to say nothing and to write nothing that did not express his deepest thought
remains for the survivors an object of in-
conclusive debate. The sincerity of a
man makes him more mysterious to us.
Jacques Rivière's body has reposed for a
year on the slopes of the hill of Cénon,
facing the town where we were both born;
but his soul full of enigmas dwells among
us, like a contradictory sign. As in the case
of Arthur Rimbaud who guides certain
young men of to-day toward death and
formerly opened the portals of Heaven for
Claudel, it is because not a single word of
his remains that does not express com-

pletely what he was at the moment he
wrote it. The unity of a Rimbaud or of a
Rivière rests not in a fixed system, but in
the constantly faithful adherence to their
progressing thought.

*A la trace de Dieu (On the Trail of
God)*, a posthumous book by Jacques
Rivière, sets minds at variance concerning
him. We have within our grasp the secret
of that life and death, affirm some. Rivière
who, as soldier and captive, picked up the
traces of God in his life with patient joy,
and who could be afraid sometimes that he
had lost them, to-day knows that we have
found them, we, his friends. That spring
which had refreshed the soldier prisoner
had gone underground again, and he
thought himself forsaken. But to-day when
he is no longer here, we have seen that
water welling up from his tomb, and burst-
ing forth for the salvation of a multitude.
To which the others oppose the fact that
in that posthumous book they do not recognize the voice of their comrade. They

say they never knew the Rivière who wrote *A la trace de Dieu*. To hear them, unusual circumstances must have inspired those pages whose sense he would not even have understood a year before his death.

What side should we choose in such a debate, except that of accepting piously our friend's work, but the entire work like Christ's robe, without seam and indivis- ible? Not to draw him to us any more than to reject him, must we set this book apart from the heritage Rivière entrusts to us. We are sure, we who have known him, that he is altogether in each one of his books; but we are certain also that, better than any other book, *A la trace de Dieu* informs us of the contrary currents and the eddies of that beautiful river full of un- fathomed deeps and islands.

Let us first set aside the argument drawn from the circumstances under which those notes were written: between September 1914 and June 1917, Rivière, a prisoner in Germany, ill, weakened, separated from

71

everything he loved, probably felt as a slave some say, the attraction of the eternal consolation. But we think, on the contrary, that if all man's unhappiness comes from not being able to remain alone in a room, captivity may be, for those who have experienced it, an opportunity for retreat and meditation, for inner investigation. Everything that snatches us from the current and forces us to remain on the bank, enriches our spiritual life. Some of those who have experienced internment in a prison camp have spoken to us of it as a most fertile test; they recall the time when they surpassed themselves. At Konigs-bruck and Hulseberg, Jacques Rivière, in the greatest suffering, remains alone with the heavens above his head and nothing between the sky and him: "Truly thrown to God," he writes on October 4, 1914, "with all that was left within reach of me at the moment. He is the only thing that stands firm, the only thing by which I can be sure of measuring my advance." But Rivière is never more like himself than when "thrown to God," he continues at the same time to be the man attentive to what goes on within him, the man curious about his soul as it is. No more than formerly does he claim to describe any phenomenon that his mind has not brought under control. Incapable of inventing anything, he does not invent God, but picks up His trail within himself with great attention and care, His God is doubtless the *Deus absconditus*, but a God hidden as concerns cause though everywhere revealed in His grace: grace, like water flowing under the ground for a long time, suddenly bursts the surface here and there, runs over, covers everything. It is a question here less of a God apprehensible to the heart than perceptible to the mind and reason: "The Christian," says Rivière, "is a man who uses his mind as completely as possible." And elsewhere: "The Christian is not a fool who chooses to believe certain things because they do not make sense but he believes them be-

73

cause, although senseless, yet he finds them true in his experience." A *la trace de Dieu* is the study of Providence considered as a positive science.

He applies himself to it at a time when that Providence dazzles him. But he is too clear-headed not to foresee future days when, that God being no longer manifest, he will find himself once more hovering over a soul from which nothing divine crops up. Even then he had no illusions about the fragility of his method from the point of view of apologetics, and suffered because he could not impose his inner perceptions on anyone: "The Christian can not give his reasons ... they are proofs that appear only when one has already admitted what is in question. . . ." Nothing to do for others except to be on the watch for signs of divine influence in them and to teach them to recognize it: "God being a person, every conversion is a question of meeting Him."

But it is especially himself that Rivière

mistrusts, on account of that future when he will be swallowed up again in the life where a thousand human traces confuse God's footsteps within him. And so, fore-seeing this test, he writes a note on the role of the will in faith. The will in faith! For those who know Rivière, nothing is more opposed to the natural move-ment of his mind, incapable of willing any-thing except what exists in reality. What then! He knows with absolute knowledge that he will not always taste those super-natural moments "when God, as it were, substitutes Himself for our thought and renders it useless, or when, instead of in-viting us, He calls us. He occupies us." Rivière knows that some day he will fall and find himself alone again; if it be the hour of the Will let the Will make up for the absence of God; let it raise up God during the intervals. In a prophetic vision of the test that he would have to pass, our friend shows us during those reliefs, doubt profiting from our barrenness: "the great temptation of the spirit during which we are turned over to the beasts of the mind." He understands that Faith is a virtue, because it is primarily fidelity, but above all he sees that the practice of this virtue, as difficult as it is for us all, is superabundantly so for the writer.

The director of the *Nouvelle Revue Française,* a prisoner in Germany, possessed the painful certainty that a Christian would have everything to fear from the literary profession. The man who lived to describe himself, holds firmly to what in him differs from other men; he holds on to his singularity. Converted, how much originality would be left to him? His singularity is life itself. And perhaps it was already the man of letters in Rivière who secretly resisted God's work. He perceived a gulf into which someone was drawing him, and he took fright: "up to his neck in mud in the great human adventure and without desire to be pulled out of it." What writer with faith in the

supernatural, could listen with an indifferent heart to that supplication which
was inspired in our friend by the reading of Saint Theresa? "My God, take away
from me the temptation of holiness. It is
not my business. Be satisfied with a pure
and patient life that I shall make every
effort to give you. Do not deprive me of
those delightful joys that I have known
and loved so much, that I desire so greatly
to recover. Don't make a mistake. I am not
the sort needed. I am married and a father;
I am a writer. Do not tempt me with impossible things. Do not lead me into too
great suffering."

Pulled up on the bank, set aside from
life, Jacques Rivière measures with a clear
eye that mortal danger that his faith is going to fall into as soon as he has been re-
turned to the current. At the same time
that he feels a curiosity awakening in him,
a taste for things as they are, untouched
sentiments, he knows even better what a
little dried-up, clutched-at thing the love of

77

God within him is, which he compares to a plant growing on a rock. But he did not foresee that he would hardly be back in the world again, when he would encounter face to face, flattering his taste, frantic for things as they are, the great literary temptation incarnated in and ornamented with the most delightful glamour: Marcel Proust. How could Rivière escape the fascination of Proust's work? There you have the hope of Rivière, the writer, to an absurd degree; it is not much to say that Proust did not intervene, he did not alter the real; a corpse stretched out in the middle of a furnished room, the inert but attentive prey of his sensations and his memories, he let them come to him from the most distant point of his finished days, to mount the assault of his being, to proliferate at will, to nourish themselves on his substance. It is a question of willing to believe this or that! The game consists, on the contrary, of willing nothing that can alter the matter of our experience. To act upon his soul, to act upon souls, is exactly the contrary of what Proust proposes to Rivière, already too inclined to attend to his lesson. God's footsteps in a soul—better expressed as grace—that is the agent from without that disturbs experience, that alters the given facts. The novelist becomes the police agent in charge of reconstructing the crime, and who does not want God to move the corpse. Proust does not believe, or rather he never dreams of the existence of the supernatural; but the chemist Rivière who, from the time of his captivity, took such care to follow their route, to pick up the trails, and who applied himself to defining God's wiles, who wanted to help us see, in the events of our lives, a conduct, a premeditation—by what brusque turnabout do we see him again a prey to the demon of literary curiosity, consecrated to investigations of himself that do not tend toward salvation but to a disinterested and sterile knowledge—that no longer turn toward love?

And yet that love continues to exist; God's footsteps are not effaced on our inner roads; we cover them with dust or mud, but they are not wiped out. Following certain circumstances, Rivière felt himself forsaken, betrayed even by the Infinite Being to Whom, nevertheless, he continued to pray each evening up to his last illness. If we dared to apply a term of comedy to that metaphysical debate, we would risk: *lover's quarrel.* "No other religion," he wrote, "interposes, between the faithful and God, love, with its great disorders, its extravagant logic, all the disturbances it introduces into souls. That is what makes the incomparable originality of Christianity and its unique profundity." What Proust when speaking of human love calls the intermittances of the heart, exists also in the life of grace, on God's side, only in appearance . . . but on ours! On his days of refusal, Rivière would have it that happiness was elsewhere, and I recall his childish envy one evening when I was pointing out to him on the Champs-Elysées, a young man bareheaded and driving a Delage.

Let Jacques Rivière's friends avoid choosing from his life and works what flat-ters their particular taste; let them consider rather, from his adolescence, from the time of his letters to Claudel, up to his death agony when he felt the approach of an overwhelming happiness, the movements of a soul, in turn attracted and repelled, adoring or grumbling, but always as sub-missive to God's action as the moon is to ebb and flow.

And finally let them ask themselves if in any other work of Rivière's, we find, as in *A la trace de Dieu,* that harrowing accent of purity, of candor, of childlikeness—as when meditating on death he remembers his mother: "The death of Mama, waiting with all her last strength for my return from school to kiss me, and to have me with her too at this last hour that she might present herself to God with me both in thought and in her eyes." There is doubtless another Rivière unhealthily attached like all of us novelists to what passes, and turning his back on what will not pass away; but there was, and there will always be, that simple studious child, with his schoolbag full of books; and I see him on his return from school, freed from all that paper and ink; and, standing on the thresh-old of light, his mother, Alain Fournier, Péguy, who cry out to him: "You are saved, Jacques, you hold the discovery in your grasp!"

JACQUES RIVIÈRE'S LETTERS

Jacques Rivière's case brings us back to the problem which was our generation's— that of sincerity. It presents itself only to a small number of Christians; the greater part never question the principles they received in school; from childhood they inclined the automaton and repeated the formulas; their natures are entirely made up of that habit. With the most fervent of them, the mechanism of their spiritual life stiffens itself against all self-examination. The slightest stirring of uncertainty, a question that comes to their mind, is written down immediately under the heading of pride, blasphemy, temptations against the faith. The intermittences of Grace, God's silences, barrenness, everything enters into an order accepted once and for all.

83

That supreme test of the Saints, that of
little Sister Theresa, during her last illness,
the complete loss of faith which no longer
survives except under its most wilful and
deliberate aspect, even that is put into the
ranks of tests reserved for great souls. The
most ordinary Christian would not even
allow himself Christ's last question to his
Father: "Why have you abandoned me?"
The system teaches them why they are
abandoned. There is nothing that does not
receive an interpretation within the general line of doctrine.

Other minds resist all that appears so
natural to most believers and revolt against
it by their very nature, although they are
everywhere open to mystical influences,
and even more sensitive than the others to
God's presence. But at certain hours only.
They do not interpret the different states
that pass through their souls, they verify
them. God is God; barrenness is barrenness; passion is passion.

Passion does not appear to them under

the guise of the adversary whom one either resists or to whom one yields, but as some-thing that is and that is not able not to be, just like that God by Whom they were possessed yesterday, and Whom they will find again to-morrow perhaps.

Jacques Rivière's letters that I publish date from the last months of his life. From 1914 to 1918 he had passed through the hell of captivity, and God had visited him in prison; or rather, forced by the circum-stances themselves to live turned inward on himself, he had had no other recourse than to pick up the divine traces in his own heart. But scarcely was he free than the outside world crowded anew into that heart emptied for years of all that was not God. The eternal was submerged there by the ephemeral, by creatures at first (espe-cially by woman whom he discovered at an age when so many others expected nothing more of her but pleasure), but also by literary work in its most dangerous form, Marcel Proust's, which has no other

85

object than itself, and whose analysis pul-
verizes and destroys the human personality.

God Who occupied Rivière the prisoner
retires, and the director of the *Nouvelle
Revue Française,* is now given over to
other forces against which he will not defend himself now any more than formerly
he defended himself against God. When
Rivière writes me that the Christian in him
is suppressed by his will-power alone, by
his reflection alone, and when he thanks
me for recalling to him that grace exists, it
is a last manifestation of the grace that sub-
sists in him, and that nature is dominating
a little more each day. Beginning with the
following letter, he recovers himself and
demands for his book and also for himself
the title of *reflective man.* We understand
what he means by that: that sort of reflection that questions everything, that ob-
serves what is, without claiming to change
anything in the heart to which he applies
it. Jacques Rivière knows very well there is

no worse offense since Christianity demands death in us, and the assassination
of the old Adam, the creation of a new
Adam in whom everything is made over,
recomposed, including attitudes, gestures
and language. Since he has taken the direction of conforming himself to the exigencies of God, Rivière must first make an
effort to conform to those of the natural
life; whence that tone, liberated and a little
affected in his last letters. That did not
prevent a novel from interesting him at
that time to the extent that he found in it
a hint of struggle against the angel; it is a
sign that it was only interrupted in him,
and that he remained harrowed by that
secret struggle.

Even when a boy, born Catholic and
French like Jacques Rivière, takes the side
of humanism, it is really a side that he
takes; that is to say, he is torn in half; one
side of him protests and debates. That art
of leading his reflection and his life freely
without taking any account of religion, or

87

feeling any embarrassment because he belongs to it (honored, nevertheless, and even practiced, but on a plane considered beyond the grasp of the intelligence), the art which was Montaigne's, that was what Rivière was, doubtless, the least capable of. "The human mind stands ever in perplexity," writes Emerson, "demanding intellect, demanding sanctity, impatient equally of each without the other. The reconciler has not yet appeared."

Jacques Rivière aspired to the domination of that discontent at the end of his life. He had searched for the reconciler in all the masters who, one after the other, had disappointed his adolescence. With the passing of his tormented youth, he no longer counted on anything but the law which he received from himself. "I am frightfully autonomous," he wrote me. He thought he was; but approaching death was going to impose the supreme renunciation on his autonomy and submit him harshly to Another's law, that Other

Whom he had never renounced. Some weeks before his death (it is Ramon Fernandez who reports it) he protested that he had not renounced God . . . nor God Jacques Rivière.

Paris, February 16.

My dear friend,

I have just reread the proofs of the last part of your Fleuve de Feu. *I take back all the criticism that I made to you in regard to it. It is very good as it is. And I have a stronger proof of this than what any reasoning could furnish me: namely, the state of emotion in which I find myself.*

The first time, as a matter of fact, I was held back and bothered by another subject than the one you wanted to treat and which had substituted itself for it in my mind; the subject was entirely human; it was Gisèle fought over by Daniel Trasis and Madame de Villeron. You sketched that struggle of two beings around a soul and for that soul but you yourself refused

89

to bring it to fulfillment, to its maximum
intensity, since you attributed to man that
nostalgia for purity that dooms him in advance to failure, since, on the other hand,
you show Lucile pierced by the doubt and
torpor that diminish her will-power, her
activity and her influence.

Yes, the drama such as you have conceived it is, properly speaking, religious,
and you succeeded in giving it, on that
plane, a splendid reality. Massis is, perhaps,
right; maybe there is in me a religious being repressed (but not by Gide, by my will-
power alone, or rather by my reflection
which is much more serious). In sum, that
is why, at first reading, I did not want to
understand your novel. The force you put
on the stage, Grace, to call it openly by its
name, I had believed in spontaneously for
a long time, then (it is the war that did it
to me; I felt myself too forsaken) I decided
to consider them as not having occurred,
not to recognize them any more. I know
that what I am saying here is atrocious.

and surpasses natural atheism in impiety; but with me, when the mind is deceived, I mean when what it had believed true seems to steal away, there is born in its stead a formidable, frightful resentment which pushes it toward extreme scepticism.

However that may be, my first resist-ence to your dénouement evidently had its origin in that will not to believe in Grace. It gives way now that the evidence forces me to see what you wanted to do, what you have done.

My dear Mauríac, it is possible that you appear to certain Catholics as a perverted being and an evil genius; as for me, for the time being, you serve me as a good coun-cilor; you recall to me the existence of my better self that evidently I have made great efforts to forget, that life also—to my credit it must be said—has worked hard to stifle in me.

The book I have in my mind at this time, and in which there will not be an indecent or blasphemous line, is more terrible than

91

all the Immoralistes *in the world. If I suc-
ceed in not writing it, something that, in
certain respects, I deeply hope, it is to you
I shall owe it, to your example, to the dem-
onstration you furnish me, in the only form
that it can strike me now, of all the resources, of all the depths there are in the
Christian conception of the world and of
life.*

Cordially yours,

Jacques Rivière.

P.S.—*I know a Gisèle de Plailly—without Grace—but very touching too. That is
why your book touched me so much at
once. All the same, how interesting women are! Your defense of G. is admirable.
But, between you and me, it is very difficult for me to defend, as a writer and novelist, someone who does not like women.
G. will never be great, for lack of that
love, don't you think so?*

*If you consent, I will write the notice of
your book when it appears*

April 6.

My dear friend,

If I have been a long time answering you, don't be angry with me. Your letter gave me so much pleasure! But I am a regular galley-slave, and when I come from dictating thirty letters to ask for notices or refuse manuscripts, you can guess in what mood I am to write to my friends. Then I had to write an article on politics. A fine piece of work!

And still again, I had the affair Boissard-Romaine, the affair Salmon-Cl.-R. Marx, the affair Breton-Rivière, the affair Waldo Frank-Valéry Larbaud. It is frightful how small and tiresome writers can be!

We shall speak of Bourget again. If I asked you for the article, it is because I did not necessarily consider him "ferocious." It seems to me there could be a few little things to say in favor of the good man, even if there are many others with which to overwhelm him.

93

Besides, I must admit his work is almost unknown to me.

As for the notice on Marsan, there is still time. I consent to a longer time than I first gave you; would you like until the twelfth? And if that still seems too short for you, well, you can write the notice for the next number. Unless you dislike the book. But there are many fine things in it.

I should tell you that I had some regrets for the dramatic manner in which I spoke to you of my next book. In the last analysis, it was a little ridiculous. Is it really as terrible as I gave you to think? Not, at any rate, in the way you might think: by the indecency or impiety of the sentiments that I have confessed in it. No, if I gave it a subtitle—something that I shall not do— it would simply be: Life History of a Reflective Man. And indicated there is the only scandal that you must expect to find in it; the scandal that can be born of a perfectly tranquil and objective reflection on oneself, and the adaptation of a being to the exigencies of life. You see that my theme has nothing demoniacal about it, and that it is made to disappoint Massis.

I am beginning to have a horror of drama, at least of the kind that one super-adds to his inner difficulties to magnify them, to make something interesting out of them. I am beginning to find out that plea-sure and happiness, if one can arrange so as to attain them, are the most interesting things to be had in the world. I am almost ashamed of all the time I have passed in telling myself that happiness was impos-sible. It was cowardice.

There, my dear friend, you have the sense, and the only sense, in which I am be-coming impious, and that is the only de-clivity from which I was thinking of hav-ing you hold me back. But is a man ever held back from that inner declivity, even by the help of the most devoted friends? In the final analysis, if I have been very lonely until now, it is because I am fright-fully autonomous.

Yes, do not fail to show me your poetry. I think that Gallimard would accept it with pleasure as a booklet (in the collection: A work, a portrait).

Goodbye for the present. I thank you again for your letter, and for the friendship you show for me. Very affectionately yours,

Jacques Rivière.

January 4.

My dear friend,

I have finally read Genitrix. I do not have the book handy as I left it with Gide whom one casual glance at it enticed.

You know how much I like everything you are doing now; this new book is no exception. Why had Jaloux' article made me think it was so different from what I found it to be? I found it at the same time simpler, more unilinear, more moulded, if I dare say so.

Your leisurely composition, your wise

96

manner of retailing the past by little snatches interspersed into the present, your way of overtaking life wherever it suits you, where it appears to you, pleases me infinitely in certain respects. This always allows you to be concrete, clear, and it reproduces admirably the manner in which, in practice, we learn the story, from both ends, as it were.

But that also upsets somewhat my mind which is morbidly in love with continuity. I should like to grasp from inside, follow with a glance that nothing would distract, the relationship between the mother and son. I half see it, I have some feeling about it, but too many elements remain hidden from me, escape even hypotheses. It is the same for the son's passion for Mathilde, after she is dead.

I know I am tiresome and indiscreet. But take good account of all the interest that this indiscretion bears for your characters and your work.

They live, my dear friend, since I should

like to know more about them. They live;
and that is the important point.

Your beginning is magnificent. The precision of the atmosphere is almost dizzying.
And the mind remains impregnated by it
to the point that I never pick up your book
again from my shelves without immediately smelling the odor of coal and syringa.

I pour out my impressions to you hur-
riedly and in disorder; but you know how
weighed down I am by my work.

I hope to see you soon. We shall only
be gone Wednesday, the 16th. (I am going to Belgium.) I am waiting for your
notices on Métérie et Idéologues. Short,
please.—Thank you! I am very happy to
have a Cahier Vert of your Genitrix. You
were very kind to save me one. I am

Your friend,

J. R.

Domaine de Saint-Victor,
Cénon (Gironde).
September 12.

My dear François,

I thank you for your notice, excellent in spite of the bad conditions under which you say you had to write it. You were right to bring out that second Madame de Noilles whom one does not notice sufficiently, or at any rate does not distinguish enough from the gardener and the ecstatic one. Nevertheless, may I say to you that my enthusiasm even for the second remains a little more hesitant than yours?

I told you, I believe, how anxious I was to get acquainted with your new novel. Your development as a novelist is the one that interests me most to-day; it is the most dramatic that I know; your progress is always surprising, in the strongest sense of the word. When can I read something?

I no longer remember what you told me about its publication in a magazine. But if it has not yet been taken, the N. R. F.

*would most enthusiastically place its can-
didacy for the honor of undertaking it.
I won't write a preface for you, you know,
because it seems that when I do, they only
"snuff out" the good of the article.**

　　　Your sincere friend,

　　　　　Jacques Rivière.

*P.S.—Where should I send you the
proofs of your notice?*

　　　　　Monday evening.

My dear François,

*I am profiting by a moment's leisure to
begin to give you my detailed impression
of your novel; but as I am dead-tired, per-
mit me to use the most commonplace style.*

*This time you did it. I felt a little shiver
at the beginning of the fourth part (conversation between Raymond and Maria at
the bar). I thought it was going to turn to
simple, melancholy reminiscences of the
past, like Jaloux'. But not at all! The fol-*

---

*There is a play on words here impossible to render in English.
Chapeau, a hat, is contrasted with éteignoir, a snuffer (dunce-cap).
There is also the idea of the preface as similar to the lifting of the
hat, in that both are acts of courtesy. (Translator's note.)

100

lowing scenes surge up magnificently, and the last between the father and son is splendid. It is a novel, a real one.

I, whose profession and perhaps gift it is, to see directly into the minds of crea-tures, see very well all there is of you in it, all the scraps of your soul that you have abandoned to it. But that is because it is my profession. The work, in reality, is completely detached from you, and lives its own personal life. All your characters are constructed to the last detail. There is not a trace of that slackness of imagination which sometimes held you back in the pre-ceding ones, and which produced dead parts, or rather parts of the author, where the author alone was active. In Le Désert de l'Amour, the action is absolutely every-where characteristic of the characters; you had the patience to allow each of them to secrete his acts and thoughts very com-pletely.

There is also very remarkable composi-tion; I mean . . . that the elements are utilized with the most happy economy. . . .

(I stop on this point; I can not develop
my thought very well.)

But, yes, I can; the lives of the characters evolve in a manner at the same time
distinct and perfectly combined; there is
that reciprocal repercussion of one on the
other that is indispensible if there is to be
a novel, and yet each one can be seen de-
veloping in his own desert. I do not know
how you succeeded in doing that, but it is
a remarkable success.

CONCLUSION

He sent me the letter that weariness had prevented his finishing. Simple weariness, he said, and it was the approach of death.

More than twenty years have passed over that tomb in the cemetery of Cénon where he reposes above the curving river that saw the birth of both of us. And we scarcely understand to-day how the disagreement arose between the wife who was right to protest that Jacques had fallen asleep in the Lord, and his humanist friends who were not altogether wrong in maintaining that he had been, during the last months, such as the letters he addressed to me show him: devoted to discoveries of every kind that a life indifferent to divine things reserved for him. Conflicts of that order give proof of the simplicity of mind of people whose profession it is to be subtle, and who have the idea that a "converted man" is a man determined for all time, petrified into an attitude to which he remains faithful; or if he renounces it some day, it is to come back to his former life. In reality, we know grace does not destroy nature, and that "the diverse movements of nature and of grace," to speak like the *Imitation,* continue the rhythm of the whole Christian life; and that it is sometimes grace, and sometimes nature that wins the victory. Jacques Rivière was, like every one of us Christians, the enclosed field where that doubtful combat takes place, yes, doubtful up to the last second, the last sigh. But his sincerity toward himself, the need that he had to leave nothing in obscurity manifested openly the ups and downs of that struggle that most Christians hide inside themselves. The state of grace is not a stable one except among the Saints; in the ordinary Christian, it is rather like that love, taciturn and always

104

menaced, of which Vigny speaks. It is a flame that the wind of the earth excites and, at the same time, is likely to put out at any moment. Grace in Jacques threw off sparks. In how many lives have there only been moments of grace! And all our inner story tends toward an effort to diminish the intervals between those times of light, so that the end of our lives re-sembles those long June twilights, when all night long the light remains in the lower part of the sky.

105

www.ingramcontent.com/pod-product-compliance
Lightning Source LLC
Chambersburg PA
CBHW051839040426
42447CB00006B/611